WHAT ARE STATE AND LOCAL GOVERNMENTS?

SARAH MACHAJEWSKI

Britannica®
Educational Publishing

IN ASSOCIATION WITH

ROSEN
EDUCATIONAL SERVICES

Published in 2016 by Britannica Educational Publishing (a trademark of Encyclopædia Britannica, Inc.) in association with The Rosen Publishing Group, Inc.
29 East 21st Street, New York, NY 10010

Distributed exclusively by Rosen Publishing.
To see additional Britannica Educational Publishing titles, go to rosenpublishing.com.

First Edition

Britannica Educational Publishing
J. E. Luebering: Director, Core Reference Group
Mary Rose McCudden: Editor, Britannica Student Encyclopedia

Rosen Publishing
Hope Lourie Killcoyne: Executive Editor
Christine Poolos: Editor
Nelson Sá: Art Director
Danijah Brevard: Designer
Cindy Reiman: Photography Manager

Library of Congress Cataloging-in-Publication Data

Machajewski, Sarah.
What are state and local governments?/Sarah Machajewski.
     pages cm. — (Let's find out! Government)
Includes bibliographical references and index.
ISBN 978-1-62275-986-6 (library bound) — ISBN 978-1-62275-987-3 (pbk.) —
ISBN 978-1-62275-989-7 (6-pack)
1. State governments — United States — Juvenile literature. 2. Local government — United States — Juvenile literature. I. Title.
JK2408.M275 2016
320.80973 — dc23
                                                                                    2014037270

Manufactured in the United States of America

Photo credits: Cover, interior pages background image John Burdumy/Moment/Getty Images; p. 4 Panoramic Images/Getty Images; p. 5 Farrell Grehan/Science Source/Getty Images; p. 6 Brendan Smialowski/AFP/Getty Images; pp. 7, 12, 20, 21, 22 © AP Images; p. 8 Fuse/Thinkstock; p. 9 Monkey Business Images/Thinkstock; p. 10 Megan Q Daniels/First Light/Getty Images; p. 11 Tetra Images/Getty Images; p. 13 Spencer Platt/Getty Images; p. 14 Kevork Djansezian/Getty Images; p. 15 Hill Street Studios/Getty Images; p. 16 Keith Bedform/Reuters/Landov; p. 17 Portland Press Herald/Getty Images; p. 18 SuperStock/Getty Images; p. 19 Brendan Smialowski/AFP/Getty Images; pp. 23, 27 Bloomberg/Getty Images; p. 24 © The Orange County Register/ZUMA Press; p. 25 Puretock/Thinkstock; p. 26 The Washington Post/Getty Images; p. 28 © Danita Delimont/Alamy; p. 29 Tom Williams/CQ-Roll Call Group/Getty Images.

CONTENTS

GOVERNING THE PEOPLE

What do you picture when you hear the word "government"? Do you picture the president or the White House? Those are important symbols of the U.S. government, which represents the whole country. But the United States is so big that its government can't manage everything that happens

The White House in Washington, D.C., is an important symbol of the U.S. government.

4

Local government leaders hold a public meeting.

in every state, city, or town.
That's what state and local governments are for.

State and local governments function much like the federal government. They make rules and laws. They maintain important facilities used by the public. Every state even has its own constitution! Read on to learn more about state and local governments, how they work, and how they affect our lives.

LEVELS OF POWER

The United States is run by governments of various levels and sizes, ranging from local to state to national. The federal government is the highest level of government. It makes laws for the whole country. State governments are the next level. They're responsible for laws, rights, and services that aren't covered by the federal government.

President Barack Obama leads the entire federal government.

◀◀

Part of a state governor's job is to work with other governmental officials.

Local governments are a level below state governments. They're responsible for the laws and services in a particular county, city, town, or village. A local government's power is divided among people who make decisions and laws, people who carry them out, and people who make sure they are being followed.

THINK ABOUT IT

Like the federal government, local governments are divided into three branches. Why would local governments want to be structured like the national government?

What Does a Local Government Do?

If you've ever visited a park, borrowed a book from the library, or been helped by the police, you've used something managed by your local government. Local governments are also called municipal governments.

Municipal governments tailor their services based on what the people in an area need. They're

Libraries are an important service provided by our local governments.

COMPARE AND CONTRAST

Imagine a city with many children and little crime and another city with mostly adults and lots of crime. Compare and contrast the services that the local governments of these cities may provide.

in charge of police and fire departments, courts, prisons, schools, hospitals, garbage collection, water and sewage systems, parks and playgrounds, public transportation, and more.

The kinds of services a local government provides depends on how big the municipality is. Large cities have their own libraries, museums, zoos, and more. Several small towns in the same county may share their services.

Local governments make sure we have firefighters in place to help with emergencies.

Local Taxes

Local governments provide many services to their people, but the services aren't free. They're paid for by taxes. Taxes are payments to the government that are required by law. Almost every country, state, and city or town collects taxes from its citizens. Taxes are used to build schools, roads, and bridges and to pay for police and firefighting services. Taxes also pay government officials' salaries.

There are many different types of taxes. Property tax is

Taxpayers helped pay for the cost of paving these roads.

one major tax charged by local governments. People who own houses and other types of property must pay the government a tax on their property. In fact, that's where most of a local government's revenue comes from.

This couple is calculating how much tax money they owe the government.

11

Meet Your Local Government

Many local governments are run by a mayor and city council. They work together to make decisions and discuss issues that arise. The city council acts as the city's legislative branch. It proposes rules and suggests how money should be spent on projects and improvements for the town. As a city's executive branch, the mayor has the final say on what a city council proposes.

Residents of Seattle, Washington, attend a meeting of their local government.

A mayor's power is determined by law. Many mayors enforce laws, manage services, and oversee budgets and projects. In some cases, the mayor may lead a city council, but the city council holds most of the power.

THINK ABOUT IT

The mayor and the city council work together to make decisions and carry out laws. Why is this balance of power important?

ELECTING LOCAL LEADERS

How does someone become a mayor or councilmember? In most cases, people vote for their leaders during an election. Voting is a process in which citizens choose who they think will do the best job.

The people who run for positions in government are called candidates. In order to win, candidates must convince voters they are the right choice. They do this by giving speeches, meeting with voters, and sponsoring

This candidate campaigns to be the mayor of Los Angeles, California.

Voters go to the polls on Election Day to choose their leaders.

advertisements on television and radio. They often address problems and needs that are very important to residents. On Election Day, the candidate with the most votes wins. The length of the term depends on the local laws.

COMPARE AND CONTRAST

Local officials are elected by the people. The president is elected by the people, too. Compare and contrast local elections with national elections.

GETTING INVOLVED

Local governments work best when they meet the needs of the people they serve. It is important for residents to let officials know what they want. There are plenty of ways for kids to get involved. Start by visiting your city hall. Check your town's website for news about your local government.

Students meet with the mayors of New York City and Ottawa, Canada.

Telling your government what you want is a great way to get involved.

Want to do more? Become familiar with what's happening in your town. Reading the newspaper and talking to other residents are great ways to learn how people feel. If you want to voice your opinion, you can attend town hall meetings and public rallies, write letters to your local officials, and more.

Think About It

Voting is a great way to help make changes in your community, but citizens can't vote until they are 18 years old. If you are too young to vote, what are other ways to make your voice heard?

THE FEDERAL SYSTEM

The United States has a federal system of government. That means there is a balance of power between the large central government and smaller state governments. The people who formed the country also had to balance power among the states themselves so that no state would have more power than the others.

Federal and state governments have worked together since the late 1700s, when the United States was formed.

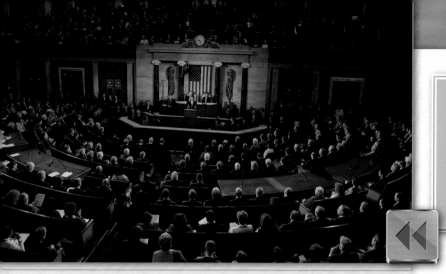

One way they did this was by creating a legislature with two houses — the Senate and the House of Representatives. The Senate and the House of Representatives make up the United States Congress. Each state elects two senators to the Senate. A state's population determines how many representatives it has in the House.

COMPARE AND CONTRAST

Every state is represented equally in the Senate, but states with large populations have more members in the House of Representatives than less-populated states. Compare and contrast the balance of power in the two houses.

How a State Is Run

Like the federal government, every state government has an executive, legislative, and judicial branch. The governor is the executive branch. The legislative branch is called different things in different states. Some legislatures are called the general assembly. In other cases they are called the state legislature. Most consist of two houses, as at the federal level. The courts make up the judicial branch. The three branches work together to make decisions for a state.

Minnesota's state governor signs a bill into law.

State supreme court judges hear arguments related to state law.

Ideas for **legislation** are first brought to state representatives. They turn the idea into a bill. The bill is then presented to

VOCABULARY

Legislation is a law that has been enacted by a governing body. It also refers to the process of making a law.

the whole legislature for debate. If the bill is passed, the governor can either sign the bill and create a law or veto it. The state supreme court hears challenges to these laws. The judges can uphold them or go against them.

States' Rights

The U.S. Constitution does not give the states clear powers. According to the Constitution, states cannot create their own currency. They cannot have their own army or navy, and they cannot enter into treaties with foreign countries. States must recognize other states' laws, and visitors are entitled to the same rights as a state's citizens.

If the Constitution does not clearly say that the federal

The Tenth Amendment to the Constitution guarantees states' rights.

THINK ABOUT IT

Why is it important that states have the power to make their own laws, separate from the federal government?

government has power over an issue, the power is given to the state. This is why states are allowed to create their own laws. These laws are contained in a state's constitution, which spells out the rights of the government and its citizens.

State governments have the power to make laws based on what the people want.

FOR THE PEOPLE

State governments stay very busy. They are in charge of running a whole state! State governments provide help to people who need food, housing, or health care. They manage state schools and hospitals and

The Department of Motor Vehicles is run by the state.

make laws to protect a state's air, land, and water. State governments also grant drivers' licenses and maintain the state police.

States pay for these services by taxing citizens. State residents may pay an **income tax** and sometimes a **sales tax.** The state government collects these taxes and then uses the money to pay for things. State governments try to give a balanced amount of money to all their services and institutions.

Some states collect a tax on purchases citizens make at stores.

STATE LEADERS

Like other local leaders, state officials are chosen during an election. Residents vote for the candidate they think will do the best job in office. They may select someone who shares the same view on important issues or someone who promises to change something they're unhappy with.

State leaders must get to know the citizens they represent in order to succeed in office.

The term lengths for elected officials vary from state to state. Most governors, state senators, and

Government officials meet to discuss important issues affecting their state.

state representatives are elected for terms that last for two to four years. Other state officials include the state attorney general, judges, secretary of state, and commissioners.

COMPARE AND CONTRAST

Candidates for local government have to campaign only in their city, while candidates for state government must reach voters across the whole state. Compare and contrast what candidates must do at each level.

YOU AND YOUR GOVERNMENT

Every government runs differently, so it's important to learn the laws and rights granted to you by your state. If you live near your state capital, plan a visit to the capitol building or courthouses. Or check out your state government's website. Read about your leaders and issues that concern residents like you. If there is an issue you feel strongly about, write a letter

You can visit and tour your state capitol building or courthouse.

No matter what your age, you can get involved in government.

to your governor or congresspersons. It's important to make your voice heard!

Getting involved with your state and local governments is a great way to see government at work. You'll become familiar with our country's systems of government and what it means to be a citizen of the United States.

THINK ABOUT IT
How do the three levels of government work together to serve the people?

Glossary

campaign To work in an organized way toward a goal, such as getting elected to public office.

citizen A full member of a country, state, or town.

constitution A written set of laws.

determine To cause something to occur in a particular way.

elect To vote into office.

function To work or operate in a certain way.

judicial branch The branch of government that interprets laws.

legislative branch The branch of government that makes laws.

legislature The legislative body of a country or a state.

manage To be in charge of.

municipality A city or town.

opinion How a person feels about an issue.

property tax Money charged to own a property.

represent To stand for.

veto The power to reject a decision proposed by a law-making body.

FOR MORE INFORMATION

Books

Jeffries, Joyce. *Meet the Mayor.* New York, NY: Gareth Stevens Publishing, 2013.

Kenney, Karen. *State Government* (U.S. Government and Civics). Vero Beach, FL: Rourke Pub. Group, 2014.

Manning, Jack. *The State Governor* (Our Government). Mankato, MN: First Facts Books, 2014.

Sobel, Syl. *How the U.S. Government Works.* Hauppauge, NY: Barron's Educational Series, Inc., 2012.

Websites

Because of the changing nature of Internet links, Rosen Publishing has developed an online list of Web sites related to the subject of this book. This site is updated regularly. Please use this link to access the list:

http://www.rosenlinks.com/lfo/State

INDEX